The Story of
RUBY BRIDGES

WITHDRAWN

The Story of
RUBY BRIDGES

by ROBERT COLES
Illustrated by GEORGE FORD

SCHOLASTIC INC.
New York Toronto London Auckland Sydney

T 79967

Coles

1. Desegregation

To RUBY BRIDGES HALL
and to all who did as she did
for the United States of America
— R . C .

To my wife, BERNETTE,
who relived Ruby's ordeal with me
— G . F .

No part of this publication may be reproduced in whole or in part, or stored in a retrieval system, or transmitted in any form or by any means, electronic, mechanical, photocopying, recording, or otherwise, without written permission of the publisher. For information regarding permission, write to Scholastic Inc., 555 Broadway, New York, NY 10012.

ISBN 0-590-43968-5

Text copyright © 1995 by Robert Coles. Illustrations copyright © 1995 by George Ford.
All rights reserved. Published by Scholastic Inc.

12 11 10 9 8 7 6 5 4 3 2 1   7 8 9/9 0 1 2/0

Printed in the U.S.A.   14

Designed by Marijka Kostiw

George Ford used watercolor paints mixed with acrylic inks and conventional drawing inks
to create the illustrations for this book.

Our Ruby taught us all a lot.
She became someone who helped change our country.
She was part of history,
just like generals and presidents are part of history.
They're leaders, and so was Ruby.
She led us away from hate, and she led us nearer to
knowing each other,
the white folks and the black folks.

— RUBY'S MOTHER

Ruby Bridges was born in a small cabin near Tylerton, Mississippi.
"We were very poor, very, very poor," Ruby said. "My daddy worked
picking crops. We just barely got by. There were times when we
didn't have much to eat. The people who owned the land were
bringing in machines to pick the crops, so my daddy lost his job,
and that's when we had to move. I remember us leaving. I was four,
I think."

In 1957, the family moved to New Orleans. Ruby's father became a janitor. Her mother took care of the children during the day. After they were tucked in bed, Ruby's mother went to work scrubbing floors in a bank.

Every Sunday, the family went to church.

"We wanted our children to be near God's spirit," Ruby's mother said. "We wanted them to start feeling close to Him from the very start."

At that time, black children and white children went to separate schools in New Orleans. The black children were not able to receive the same education as the white children. It wasn't fair. And it was against the nation's law.

In 1960, a judge ordered four black girls to go to two white elementary schools. Three of the girls were sent to McDonogh 19. Six-year-old Ruby Bridges was sent to first grade in the William Frantz Elementary School.

Ruby's parents were proud that their daughter had been chosen to take part in an important event in American history. They went to church.

"We sat there and prayed to God," Ruby's mother said, "that we'd all be strong and we'd have courage and we'd get through any trouble; and Ruby would be a good girl and she'd hold her head up high and be a credit to her own people and a credit to all the American people. We prayed long and we prayed hard."

On Ruby's first day, a large crowd of angry white people gathered outside the Frantz Elementary School. The people carried signs that said they didn't want black children in a white school. People called Ruby names; some wanted to hurt her. The city and state police did not help Ruby.

The President of the United States ordered federal marshals to walk with Ruby into the school building. The marshals carried guns.

Every day, for weeks that turned into months, Ruby experienced that kind of school day.

She walked to the Frantz School surrounded by marshals. Wearing a clean dress and a bow in her hair and carrying her lunch pail, Ruby walked slowly for the first few blocks. As Ruby approached the school, she saw a crowd of people marching up and down the street. Men and women and children shouted at her. They pushed toward her. The marshals kept them from Ruby by threatening to arrest them.

Ruby would hurry through the crowd and not say a word.

The white people in the neighborhood would not send their children to school. When Ruby got inside the building, she was all alone except for her teacher, Miss Hurley. There were no other children to keep Ruby company, to play with and learn with, to eat lunch with.

But every day, Ruby went into the classroom with a big smile on her face, ready to get down to the business of learning.

"She was polite and she worked well at her desk," Miss Hurley said. "She enjoyed her time there. She didn't seem nervous or anxious or irritable or scared. She seemed as normal and relaxed as any child I've ever taught."

So Ruby began learning how to read and write in an empty classroom, an empty building.

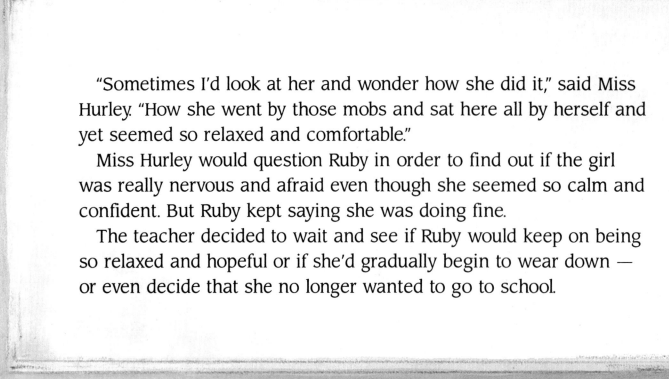

"Sometimes I'd look at her and wonder how she did it," said Miss Hurley. "How she went by those mobs and sat here all by herself and yet seemed so relaxed and comfortable."

Miss Hurley would question Ruby in order to find out if the girl was really nervous and afraid even though she seemed so calm and confident. But Ruby kept saying she was doing fine.

The teacher decided to wait and see if Ruby would keep on being so relaxed and hopeful or if she'd gradually begin to wear down — or even decide that she no longer wanted to go to school.

Then one morning, something happened. Miss Hurley stood by a window in her classroom as she usually did, watching Ruby walk toward the school. Suddenly, Ruby stopped — right in front of the mob of howling and screaming people. She stood there facing all those men and women. She seemed to be talking to them.

Miss Hurley saw Ruby's lips moving and wondered what Ruby could be saying.

The crowd seemed ready to kill her.

The marshals were frightened. They tried to persuade Ruby to move along. They tried to hurry her into the school, but Ruby wouldn't budge.

Then Ruby stopped talking and walked into the school.

When she went into the classroom, Miss Hurley asked her what happened. Miss Hurley told Ruby that she'd been watching and that she was surprised when Ruby stopped and talked with the people in the mob.

Ruby became irritated.

"I didn't stop and talk with them," she said.

"Ruby, I saw you talking," Miss Hurley said. "I saw your lips moving."

"I wasn't talking," said Ruby. "I was praying. I was praying for them."

Every morning, Ruby had stopped a few blocks away from school to say a prayer for the people who hated her. This morning she forgot until she was already in the middle of the angry mob.

When school was over for the day, Ruby hurried through the mob as usual. After she walked a few blocks and the crowd was behind her, Ruby said the prayer she repeated twice a day — before and after school:

Please, God, try to forgive those people.
Because even if they say those bad things,
They don't know what they're doing.
So You could forgive them,
Just like You did those folks a long time ago
When they said terrible things about You.

AFTERWORD

Later that year, two white boys joined Ruby at the Frantz Elementary School. Their parents were tired of seeing the boys get into mischief around the house when they could have been in school and learning. The mob became very angry when the first white boys went back to school. But those boys were soon joined by other children.

"We've been sitting back and letting our children get cheated out of an education because some people have tried to take the law into their own hands," one parent said. "It's time for us to fight for the side of the law and for our children's right to go to a school and get their education."

They all did get their education, Ruby and a growing number of boys and girls who went to school with her. By the time Ruby was in the second grade, the mobs had given up their struggle to scare Ruby and defeat the federal judge's order that New Orleans schools be desegregated so that children of all races might be in the same classroom. Year after year, Ruby went to the Frantz School. She graduated from it, then went on to graduate from high school.

Ruby Bridges is married to a building contractor and has four sons who attend school within the New Orleans Public School System. Now a successful businesswoman, she has created the Ruby Bridges Educational Foundation for the purpose of increasing parental involvement in schools. For further information about the foundation, write to the following address: The Ruby Bridges Educational Foundation, P.O. Box 870248, New Orleans, Louisiana 70187.

About the Author

Dr. Robert Coles is a child psychiatrist who has worked with young people in various parts of America; he is a Pulitzer Prize-winning author. He received his A.B. from Harvard University and his M.D. from Columbia University College of Physicians and Surgeons.

Dr. Coles is a research psychiatrist for the Harvard University Health Services. His distinguished list of books for adults includes *Children of Crisis* (in five volumes); *The Political Life of Children*; and *The Moral Life of Children*. He lives with his family outside Boston, Massachusetts.

About the Illustrator

George Ford has illustrated many books, two of which have received prestigious literary awards. *Ray Charles*, by Sharon Bell Mathis, was honored with the Coretta Scott King Award, and *Paul Robeson*, by Eloise Greenfield, was given the Jane Addams Children's Book Award.

Other books he has illustrated include *Bright Eyes, Brown Skin*, by Cheryl Willis Hudson and Bernette G. Ford, and *Jamal's Busy Day*, by Wade Hudson. Mr. Ford lives with his wife and daughter in Brooklyn, New York.